For Declan, with love

One
Nation Under God

When America was not yet born,
    We needed faith to guide us,
To help us when our hopes were worn—
    A God to stand beside us.

When our hopes began to stir,
    And when our hopes were dim,
He guided us as we became
    One nation under Him.

And when we bow our heads to pray,
    We know our prayers are heard.
America won't lose her way
    If we always heed His word.

TWO CHAMBERS

3

Two
Chambers in Congress

The Senate and House are **two** different parts,
    But working together is right at the heart
Of how laws are discussed and debated and passed
    So our government is fair and Congress will last.

The House represents parts of a state that are small,
    While the Senate looks out for each state overall
To make sure things work in each little location
    And all laws are for the good of the nation.

We give them power when we give them our vote–
    A fact which is really something of note.
And if we do not like what they do or they say,
    We send them back home on the next Election Day.

Three
Branches of Government

Power is split so our founders were able
    To be sure America's balance is stable.
Each different branch has its own job to do
    To keep government on track whatever they do.

The Legislative branch gives us our laws.
    The Judicial branch checks each one for flaws.
The Executive branch makes sure we obey.
    The **three** work together to protect us each day.

Checks and balances on each of the **three**
    To keep us safe and fair and free.
The power is divided so no one is king.
    We can govern ourselves. Let freedom ring!

Four
Presidents on Mount Rushmore

Washington reminds all those who see
    America was not always free
When independence was a fight
    Before it was one of our rights.

The people can govern, that's what Jefferson said.
    We don't need a king; we don't need to be led.
Put America's future in Americans' hands.
    We can decide for ourselves in this
        wonderful land.

Roosevelt showed that we stayed strong
    As we grew and time marched on.
He proved that, not just for today,
    America is here to stay.

Are we all equal? Are we together? we asked.
    Lincoln made sure that we rose to the task.
He made sure our progress could not be undone.
    He kept us united, kept America one.

Five
Branches in Our Military

On the water, fighting bravely,
    The seas are protected by our Navy.
The Air Force guards us in the sky,
    The engine's roar their battle cry.

Warriors arriving from the sea,
    These are our U.S. Marines.
We have our Army on the land
    When liberty must take a stand.

When near our shores there is trouble,
    The Coast Guard gets there on the double.
Five branches fight to keep us free,
    To protect us and our liberty.

Six
Ships that Kept Us Free

When America was still quite new,
    We needed our own naval crew.
Six boats with sailors strong and brave
    To protect our country on the waves.

Right away, those boats were tested.
    We fought and battled, never rested.
When the gun smoke cleared above the sea
    Our ships were there and were still free.

The pirates thought they were the best,
    They'd find and fight and capture the rest.
But they were forced into retreat
    By our bravery and our tiny fleet.

Seven Rays on the Statue of Liberty

This statue won't let us forget
    The battles fought with words and sweat,
Before Americans took a stand
    For a republic in this land.

On her crown, those **seven** rays
    Remind Americans every day
That on **seven** lands and **seven** seas
    Many still are not yet free.

She means hope for those around the world:
    Men and women, boys and girls.
For those who dream to live so free
    and those who work for liberty.

Eight
Fifes and Eight Drums

When troops marched in the Revolutionary War
    Each unit had its own fife and drum corps.
Many were boys that were too young to fight
    But their passion for freedom was burning bright.

Eight fifes and **eight** drums kept the soldiers on track
    So that each of them knew the right time to attack.
The drum's rat-a-tat-tat and the fife's toot-toot-tooting
    Was a way to tell soldiers what they should be doing.

The fluting so sweet and the drum's steady beat
    Helped our soldiers attack and made enemies retreat.
The music they played was clear, steady, and true
    And helped in the fight for the red, white, and blue.

Nine
Supreme Court Justices

If there is a law that is truly unfair,
    The Supreme Court will listen—that's why they are there.
They look at the case, they think and decide
    Using the facts to make up their minds.

They need to be clear, that's why there are **nine**.
    They all cast a vote so there can't be a tie.
Our founders created just one Supreme Court
    So that justice would stand and we couldn't fall short.

We always have problems that need to be solved
    So we look to them to get justice for all.
They work so the people will have a solution
    That is just and follows the Constitution.

NAY

Ten Amendments in the Bill of Rights

The Bill of Rights tells us that
    We may do what many can't.
So there would be no room for doubt,
    Our founding fathers laid them out.

There are **Ten** Amendments, and they mean a lot.
    They are the reasons that we fought:
Freedoms that weren't safe before,
    Freedoms well worth fighting for.

When you know you're safe in your own home,
    When you don't have to pray alone,
When you say just what you feel,
    It might not seem like a big deal.

Just remember that these rights weren't free.
    Many fought for you and me.

372.89 HAM
Hamilton, Amelia
One Nation Under God: A Book for Little Patriots
700141438